Holidays Around the World

Celebrate Halloween

Deborah Heiligman
Consultant, Dr. Jack Santino

NATIONAL GEOGRAPHIC
WASHINGTON, D.C.

Mara Bowden happily chooses a heavy pumpkin at a pumpkin patch in Tallahassee, Florida.

pumpkins

∧ Plastic jack-o'-lantern
filled with candy

In autumn, as the days get
shorter and the nights grow longer,
we get ready for Halloween. October
31 is the big day. We celebrate with
pumpkins, costumes, and candy.

costumes

People in the United States, Canada,
the British Isles, and other countries
celebrate Halloween. It comes from
an ancient holiday.

candy

∧ Candy corn

Long, long ago, Celtic people who lived in Ireland, Scotland, and England had their most important holiday around October 31. It was called Samhain (SAH-ween). The Celts believed that on this night people who had died crossed over into the other world. The Celts lit bonfires to help the dead make their journey.

People celebrate with bonfires today, too. This one is in Wiltshire, England.

The Celts lit bonfires.

Many centuries later, the leader of the Catholic Church, the Pope, named November 1 All Saints, or All Hallows, Day. "Hallow" is the old word for "saint." The night before All Hallows Day was called All Hallows Eve. This was shortened to "Halloween."

Children and adults

started dressing up.

∧ Nicolas Ramose tromps through 8,000 pumpkins lined up in the Trocadero Gardens in Paris, France, during a Halloween event.

< A "witch" and his mom get ready to trick-or-treat in London, England.

The Pope and other church leaders wanted Halloween to be a holy night, but Celtic traditions remained. And over the years more customs were added. People put out food and drink for wandering spirits, or ghosts, and for other spooky creatures said to be about. Children and adults started dressing up as those creatures and doing tricks so they could get goodies, too.

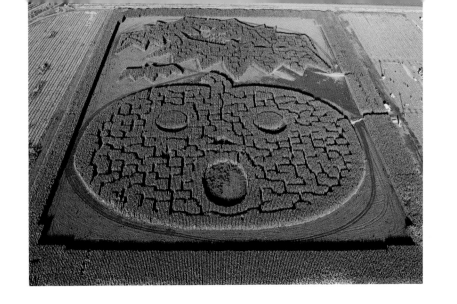

< Wouldn't you like to run around in this cornfield maze in Stockton, California?

We visit pumpkin

patches.

Since Halloween falls during harvest time, customs from harvest festivals also became part of Halloween. That's why we go apple-picking, drink apple cider, bob for apples, decorate with gourds, visit pumpkin patches, and go on hayrides.

We carve pumpkins into

jack-o'-lanterns, too. This tradition comes from an old legend about a man named Jack. Jack died, but he wasn't good enough to get into heaven. He was doomed to wander the earth at night forever. So he carved a large turnip and put a lighted coal inside so he could see where he was going.

∨ *Children at the Mustard Seed School in Sacramento, California, carve pumpkins for Halloween.*

We carve pumpkins.

∧ Children in Orense, Spain, parade with glowing jack-o'-lanterns.

The turnip with a lighted coal was a lantern. The "Jack of the Lantern" legend comes from England. But in many places, we carve pumpkins instead of turnips.

We get ready for Halloween

for weeks. We decorate our homes and our schools with pictures of ghosts and witches and black cats and jack-o'-lanterns.

> Fred Goehringer brushes the snow off Halloween decorations in Butte, Montana.

∨ Shelley Lysaght hangs a huge spider over the entrance to a Halloween display in Krug Park in St. Joseph, Missouri.

We get ready!

∧ Cat mask

We buy candy to give out to trick-or-treaters. We plan our trick-or-treating route. And we plan what we will be on Halloween.

We buy or make costumes for trick-or-treat night and Halloween parades and masquerade parties. What will you be this year? A goblin? A ghost? A superhero? A princess? A witch? A scary cat?

What will you
be this year?

Jessie Olson, left, who lost her home in a fire, puts together a Halloween costume with the help of her friend Amy Brown at the St. Gregory Church victims' center in San Diego, California.

On Halloween day we have so much fun. We march in Halloween parades around our schools and towns.

At school we sing Halloween songs, play games, put on plays, and have parties.

We march

∧ Hercules the pug is dressed as a pig for the Halloween Pet Parade in Coconut Grove, Florida.

> Fox Ballew is dressed as a volcano, and Scott Alpert is a superhero. Fox won the costume contest for his age group in Newhall, California.

< Claire Loomans, left, and Carter Markegard play Halloween bingo at Armatage Elementary School in Minneapolis, Minnesota.

in parades.

> In Tokyo, Japan, girls twirl batons in their school's "Hello Halloween Pumpkin Parade."

17

< Quinn Venittelli gets help from his mom as he prepares for Halloween in Jackson, New Jersey. His sister Kyra, dressed as a witch, is ready to go.

We put on

our costumes.

∧ *Girls apply creepy makeup as they prepare to work in a Halloween haunted house in Whitefish, Montana.*

< *Trick-or-treating on in-line skates? Be careful! These witches skate in Makati, the Philippines.*

As darkness comes,

we put on our costumes and head outside with other Halloween creatures.

Trick or treat!

We knock on doors. We say,

"Trick or treat!" Our friends try to guess who we are. They give us candy. We say, "Thank you," and go on our way.

We also trick-or-treat for UNICEF, an organization that helps poor children around the world. We bring a special box with us and ask our friends and neighbors to contribute money. Then we bring our boxes into school. Our teacher makes sure the money goes to UNICEF.

We play games.

We go to Halloween parties, too.
We dress in costumes. We try to guess who our friends are.

We play games, sing songs, and listen to scary stories. We go on ghost walks and visit haunted houses. We have fun and don't get too scared—it's all pretend.

< Halloween isn't just for kids. In Jacksonville, Florida, staff members Linda Cobb, left, and Patricia Brown dance in baby costumes as costumed residents watch at All Saint's Catholic Nursing Home.

∧ In Waterville, Maine, Gabriel Smith isn't clowning around as he tries to eat a doughnut on a string at a party.

< Alexandra Brewster, dressed as a genie, and Emily Salvador, in a magician costume, enjoy a Halloween party on skates in Burlington, Iowa.

Halloween is a time to get a
little scared, get dressed in a costume,
and have a lot of fun.

BOO!

Halloween is a time

to have fun.

Ellen Sartore and her dad, Joel,
have Halloween fun together in
Lincoln, Nebraska.

MORE ABOUT HALLOWEEN

Contents

Just the Facts

WHO CELEBRATES IT: Children and adults around the world, but especially in the United States, Canada, and the British Isles.

WHAT: A holiday to dress up in costumes and eat treats.

WHEN: October 31.

HOW LONG: The main celebration is one day and evening, though sometimes activities are held on the weekend nearest October 31.

RITUAL: Trick or treating; wearing costumes; carving pumpkins.

FOOD: Candy!

> *Kalinka Zaborowska tries to catch an apple at her friend Sasha Dadarria's Halloween party in London, England.*

Play Snap-Apple

In Ireland and other countries in the British Isles, a favorite game is snap-apple. You can play it, too. You can use apples, like the girls below, or doughnuts, like the boy on page 23. You will need string, enough apples (or doughnuts) for each player, and an adult to help you.

1. Wash apples. (Do not wash doughnuts.)
2. Tie strings around apples (or doughnuts).
3. Hang strings from the ceiling, a doorframe, tree branches, or even a clothesline. (Make sure the apples hang low enough for you and your guests to reach them.)
4. If you want the game to be really hard, tie a blindfold around each person.
5. Put your hands behind your back.
6. Have an adult shout "Go!"
7. Now everyone tries to take a bite out of an apple (or doughnut)—without using hands.
8. The first person to take a bite out of the apple or doughnut wins.

The Day of the Dead

In many parts of the world, people observe another holiday that falls near Halloween: the Day of the Dead. This holiday is celebrated on November 1 and 2. November 2 is also All Soul's Day, which is observed by Catholics and other Christians.

In Mexico, the Day of the Dead, or Dia de los Muertos, is very important. It is a day to honor people who have died, both recently and long ago. People in other Latin American countries celebrate this special day, too. So do people in the United States, especially in places where there are many people of Mexican heritage.

On Dia de los Muertos, people visit the graves of their dead loved ones. They decorate the gravesite with beautiful flowers, especially marigolds, and floral arrangements made for this day. Some people also make delicious food and put it around the gravesite. It is believed that the dead eat the spirit of the food, but then the living enjoy the delicious food that is left.

Some people also make an altar in their homes or in churches with offerings to the dead. This is called an *ofrenda*, or offering. They place flowers, candles, incense, holy cards, crucifixes, skulls, other icons, and some food on the altar. Some people believe that the ofrenda will draw the dead back to life so they can enjoy their family and the pleasures of being alive. After prayer, people dance, feast, and party.

All over Mexico people sell and buy toy skeletons who are dancing or playing guitar or riding horseback with beautiful young women. Children get candies in the shape of skulls called *calaveras de azucar*.

The Day of the Dead is both a serious religious holiday and a fun non-religious one. Most of all it is a time when people say that death is part of life. We will not be scared of death.

ᵛ *Liliana Seraldi makes a cross with marigold petals on her grandfather's grave at a cemetery in Mexico City, Mexico. Her mother and father are sorting flowers for Day of the Dead decorations.*

Spooky Graveyard Cake

My friend Rebecca Green says this cake is easy and fun to make and delicious to eat. Get an adult to help you bake the cake.

INGREDIENTS:
1 box cake mix, or your own easy cake recipe
1 can chocolate frosting (or homemade chocolate frosting)
oblong-shaped cookies
decorating icing

ANY OR ALL OF THE FOLLOWING:
gummy worms
candy pumpkins
candy corn
other assorted candies
marshmallow ghosts
small thin pretzel sticks
thick black licorice

1. Bake a sheet cake according to the directions on the box.

2. Cool the cake, then frost it.

3. Break cookies in half. Write "RIP" (for "rest in peace"), "Boo!" or friends' names on the cookies with the decorating icing. You can also draw ghosts or skeletons on the cookies.

4. Stick cookies in the cake as if they were gravestones.

5. Decorate the cake however you like. Here are some ideas: Scatter gummy worms and candies around. Place the marshmallow ghosts in the corners. Make a crooked fence around the cake by sticking in pretzels. Make trees by peeling the top of the licorice apart to make branches, and stick those in the cake, too.

HALLOWEEN SAFETY TIPS

Halloween is a fun holiday, but it's important to celebrate safely. For an excellent list of Halloween safety tips, go to this Web site, which is put out by the American Academy of Pediatrics: **http://www.aap.org/advocacy/ releases/octhalloween.htm.**
It's important for parents and children to review these tips together.

Find Out More

BOOKS

Those with a star (*) are especially good for children.

*Barth, Edna. *Witches, Pumpkins and Grinning Ghosts: The Story of the Halloween Symbols.* **Clarion Books, 1972.** Though this book was written a long time ago, it is a good resource for children in middle grades.

*Gibbons, Gail. *Halloween.* **Holiday House, 1984.** This is a good, clear, simple explanation of Halloween for young children.

*Greene, Carol. *The Story of Halloween.* **HarperCollins, 2004.** Halloween history, customs, and lore, for children ages 7 to 10. Very nicely illustrated by Linda Bronson.

Santino, Jack. *The Hallowed Eve: Dimensions of Culture in a Calendar Festival in Northern Ireland (Irish LIterature, History and Culture).* **University Press of Kentucky, 1998.** A look at the Irish origins of Halloween.

Santino, Jack, editor. *Halloween and Other Festivals of Life and Death.* **University of Tennessee Press, 1998.** This book was my guiding force in writing *Celebrate Halloween.* A must for any adult who wants to learn more about Halloween.

WEB SITES

ABOUT HALLOWEEN:
http://www.loc.gov/folklife/halloween.html
This site, put out by The American Folklife Center of the Library of Congress, is a really good explanation of the history of Halloween.

www.unicefusa.org/trickortreat
If you want to learn more about trick-or-treating for UNICEF, go to this site.

ABOUT THE DAY OF THE DEAD:
http://www.public.iastate.edu/~rjsalvad/ scmfaq/muertos.html
This site is about the Mexican celebration and explains the connection with the Aztecs.

http://www.azcentral.com/ent/dead/
This site, from Arizona, focuses on the celebrations in Arizona and in the United States. It includes crafts and articles about food and different events.

http://www.mexconnect.com/mex_/feature/ daydeadindex.html
A site from Mexico with a lot of information and links.

> In a supermarket in La Paz, Bolivia, a worker dressed in a costume gathers shopping baskets on Halloween.

29

Glossary

Ancient (AIN-shent): Very, very old.

Celts/Celtic (KELTS/KEL-tick or SELTS/SEL-tick): People who lived long ago in Europe, Britain, and Ireland.

Goblin: A strange-looking evil spirit that is mischievous and mean towards people.

Gourd (GORED): A fruit with a rounded shape and a hard rind. Gourds grow on vines.

Hallowed (HAL-owed): Holy.

Harvest: The time when ripened crops are gathered.

Masquerade (mass-kuh-RAID): A costume, or an event in which people are dressed in costumes.

Saint: A person honored by the Christian church because of her or his holy life.

Samhain (SAH-ween): An ancient festival of the Celts that celebrated the crossing of the dead into the other world.

Where This Book's Photos Were Taken

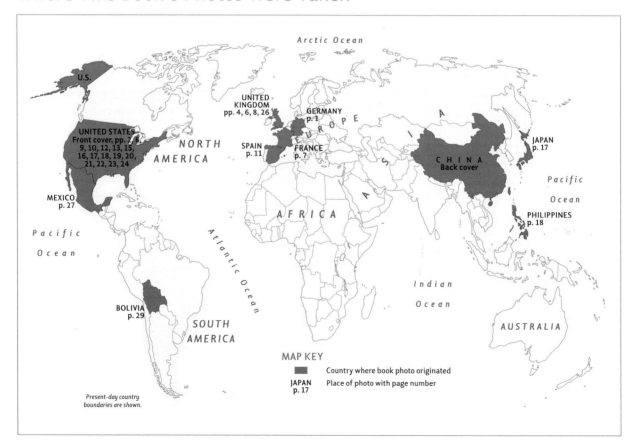

30

Halloween: A Holiday with Ancient Roots

by Dr. Jack Santino

The Halloween celebration familiar to us today has a very ancient pedigree. It can be traced back to pre-Christian festivals in Ireland, Great Britain, and Europe. The Celtic festival of Samhain is usually viewed as the festival that gave rise to Halloween. Held on November 1 (by today's calendar), Samhain was the time during which the spirits of the dead were believed to pass from this world to the next. It was also the Celtic New Year's Day and a major point of transition in the seasonal, pastoral, and agricultural calendars. In A.D. 731, after Christianity had taken hold in Ireland and Britain, November 1 was declared All Saints Day, also called All Hallows Day. The name "Halloween" derives from a contraction of "All Hallows Eve."

When I was growing up, in a neighborhood in Boston in the middle of the 20th century, Halloween was very much a children's holiday. One of my fondest memories is of the year my father taught me how to carve a pumpkin into a jack-o'-lantern. I can still smell the slimy, stringy guts we had to remove and see the finished jack aglow with a candle inside. Halloween, like any good festival, dazzles the senses.

Trick-or-treating was a journey into the unknown, as we would roam—a bit—out of our comfort zone of known neighbors to farther streets. Looking back, I believe that trick-or-treating, like many holiday customs, became a kind of rite of passage. First you went out with a family member, then proudly graduated to roaming with friends, then became too old to wear a costume, but might indulge in the pranks that were tolerated, grudgingly, on this occasion, such as tossing eggs or soaping car windows. Like the appeal to the senses, this licensed inversion—when certain taboo behavior is not only tolerated but expected—is a feature of many festivals.

In the United States, with its many different immigrant groups, the way we celebrate Halloween today is influenced by festivals and carnivals from all parts of the world. And the holiday is no longer just for children. Adults often dress in costumes, have parties with their friends, and put up elaborate decorations in their yards and homes. There are Halloween parades in cities such as New York and Washington, D.C., in which the participants mock politicians and current events with their satirical costumes.

Not everyone likes or approves of Halloween. Some people object to the occult imagery—such as devils and witches—that has become associated with Halloween over the centuries. Mexico and many European countries view the importation of the American style of celebration with alarm, as a form of economic and cultural imperialism.

Halloween is now second only to Christmas in the U.S. in terms of economic activity. Despite its commercialization, however, Halloween retains a grassroots feel. It is not an official day off from work or school. It is highly participatory. There also remains something about Halloween that speaks to the soul. Perhaps it is the connection to the harvest season, with its autumn leaves and pumpkins; perhaps it is the thrill of being outside at night, in the cool air; perhaps it is the fun of wearing masks and costumes and disguises. Perhaps it is because for once we are allowed to confront our taboos: Death, like the harvest, is part of life. Death is fearsome, to be sure, but not to be feared. The harvest sustains life, and we are all a part of this process, part of the cycle, part of nature.

Jack Santino

Jack Santino is a professor of folklore and popular culture at Bowling Green State University in Ohio. He has written several books on holidays, celebrations, and rituals, including All Around the Year: Holidays and Celebrations in American Life.

For Essie, with love.

PICTURE CREDITS

Front cover: ©John Block/Botanica/Jupiter Images; Back cover: ©Vincent Yu/Associated Press; Spine: ©Lori Sparkia/Shutterstock; 1: © Armin Weigel/dpa/Corbis; 2: ©Phil Coale/Associated Press; 3 up: ©Lori Sparkia/Shutterstock; 3 lo: ©Sandra Wood/Shutterstock; 4-5: ©ArenaPal/Topham/The Image Works; 6: ©Clare Kendall/WPN; 7: © Charles Platiau/Reuters/Corbis; 8 up: © Jim Sugar/Corbis; 8 lo: © Gerry Penny/epa/Corbis; 9: ©Jack Bland/Merced Sun-Star/Associated Press; 10: ©Leilani Hu/Sacramento Bee/ZUMA Press; 11: © Rosa Veiga/epa/Corbis; 12: © Jerry McCrea/Star Ledger/Corbis; 13 up: ©Lisa Kunkel/The Montana Standard/Associated Press; 13 lo: ©Ival Lawhon Jr./St. Joseph News-Press/Associated Press; 14 left: ©Sue/Shutterstock; 14-15: ©Lenny Ignelzi/Associated Press; 16 up: ©Amy E. Conn/Associated Press; 16 lo: ©Tom Mendoza/Los Angeles Daily News/WpN; 17 up: ©Jim Mone/Associated Press; 17 lo: © Eriko Sugita/Reuters/Corbis; 18 up: © Scott Lituchy/Star Ledger/Corbis; 18 lo: ©Alberto Marquez/Associated Press; 19: ©Robin Loznak/Daily Inter Lake /ZUMA Press; 20: ©Masterfile; 21: ©Suzanne Plunkett/Associated Press; 22: ©Jon M. Fletcher/The Florida Times-Union/ Associated Press; 23 up: ©Jim Evans/Morning Sentinel/ Associated Press; 23 lo: ©John Lovretta/The Hawk Eye/Associated Press; 24-25: ©Joel Sartore/National Geographic Image Collection; 26: ©Chris Dadarria; 27: ©Gregory Bull/Associated Press; 28: ©Aimee Gertsch; 29: ©Pablo Aneli/Associated Press.

Text copyright © 2007 Deborah Heiligman.
All rights reserved. Reproduction of the whole or any part of the contents without written permission from the National Geographic Society is strictly prohibited.

Library of Congress Cataloging-in-Publication Data

Heiligman, Deborah.
  Celebrate Halloween / Deborah Heiligman ; consultant, Jack Santino.
    p. cm. — (Holidays around the world)
  Includes bibliographical references and index.
  ISBN 978-1-4263-0120-9 (trade : alk. paper)
  ISBN 978-1-4263-0121-6 (library : alk. paper)
  1. Halloween. I. Santino, Jack. II. Title.
GT4965.H373 2007
394.2646--dc22
                        2007003121
Printed in the United States of America

Series design by 3+Co. and Jim Hiscott.
The body text in the book is set in Mrs. Eaves.
The display text is Lisboa.

Founded in 1888, the National Geographic Society is one of the largest nonprofit scientific and educational organizations in the world. It reaches more than 285 million people worldwide each month through its official journal, NATIONAL GEOGRAPHIC, and its four other magazines; the National Geographic Channel; television documentaries; radio programs; films; books; videos and DVDs; maps; and interactive media. National Geographic has funded more than 8,000 scientific research projects and supports an education program combating geographic illiteracy.

For more information, please call 1-800-NGS LINE (647-5463) or write to the following address:

National Geographic Society
1145 17th Street N.W., Washington, D.C. 20036-4688 U.S.A.

Visit us online at www.nationalgeographic.com/books

For information about special discounts for bulk purchases, please contact National Geographic Books Special Sales: ngspecsales@ngs.org

Published by the National Geographic Society
John M. Fahey, Jr., *President and Chief Executive Officer*
Gilbert M. Grosvenor, *Chairman of the Board*
Nina D. Hoffman, *Executive Vice President; President, Book Publishing Group*

STAFF FOR THIS BOOK

Nancy Laties Feresten, *Vice President, Editor-in-Chief of Children's Books*
Bea Jackson, *Design and Illustrations Director, Children's Books*
Amy Shields, *Executive Editor, Children's Books*
Marfé Ferguson Delano, *Project Editor*
Lori Epstein, *Illustrations Editor*
Melissa Brown, *Project Designer*
Carl Mehler, *Director of Maps*
Priyanka Lamichhane, *Assistant Editor*
Rebecca Baines, *Editorial Assistant*
Jennifer A. Thornton, *Managing Editor*
Gary Colbert, *Production Director*
Lewis R. Bassford, *Production Manager*
Maryclare Tracy, Nicole Elliott, *Manufacturing Managers*

Front cover: Boys dressed as pirates pose in front of a scarecrow in a New Mexico corn patch. *Back cover:* Children enjoy an early Halloween event at a shopping mall in Hong Kong, China. *Title page:* A boy lights a candle inside a huge jack-o'-lantern in Kirchroth, Germany.

ACKNOWLEDGMENTS

Thanks to Jack Santino, whose books and advice guided me in writing this book. Thanks to Marfé Ferguson Delano, who makes great pumpkin soup and knows how to roll with the punches (and graveyard cakes). Thanks also to Rebecca Green, and her mother, Julie Stockler, for the help with the graveyard cake. Thanks to all of those people who sent me disgusting and innovative recipes (sorry we couldn't use them). A special thanks to Vivian Philips and Rozanne Gold, and to Lari Robling. This book is dedicated to my sister-in-law Essie, who is the best grandma in the world (so far). Here's to many happy Halloweens with Matthew, Andrew, Katie, Owen, and PhilPa.